MAKING SENSE OF POINT OF VIEW

TRANSFORM YOUR FICTION: 1

Louise Harnby

Copyright © 2020 Louise Harnby

The right of Louise Harnby to be identified as the author of this work has been asserted by her in accordance with the Copyright, Designs and Patents Act 1988. All rights reserved. This book is sold subject to the condition that it shall not, by way of trade or otherwise, be lent, re-sold, hired out or otherwise circulated in any form of binding or cover other than that in which it is published and without a similar condition including this condition being imposed on the subsequent purchaser.

ISBN: 9798660057410

CONTENTS

1. What is narrative point of view? 1
   - Why should you bother nailing POV? 1
     - A better read 1
     - A better price 2
     - A better fix 2
   - 5 narrative viewpoint styles 2

2. First-person POV 3
   - Overview 3
   - The benefits of a first-person POV 3
   - The limitations of a first-person POV 3
   - Good practice: Not relying on 'I' 3
   - Good practice: Sustaining interest with other interpretations 5
   - Recommendation 5

3. Second-person POV 7
   - Overview 7
   - The benefits of a second-person POV 7
   - The limitations of a second-person POV 7
   - Good practice: Tension in a transgressor narrative 8
   - Good practice: Curiosity, reliability and the complicit reader 9
   - Good practice: Tight, witty prose but an acquired taste 9
   - Recommendation 10

4. Third-person limited POV 12
   - Overview 12
   - The benefits of a third-person-limited POV 12
   - The limitations of a third-person-limited POV 12

Good practice: Intimacy and getting under the character's skin	14
Good practice: Third-person limited in the present tense	15
Recommendation	15

5. Third-person objective POV — 17

- Overview — 17
- The benefits of a third-person-objective POV — 17
- The limitations of a third-person-objective POV — 18
- Good practice: A more distant and descriptive narrative — 18
- Good practice: Shown-not-told narratives in action — 19
- Good practice: Blending objective and limited — 20
- Good practice: Tension-filled objective prose — 21
- Recommendation — 21

6. Third-person omniscient POV — 22

- Overview — 22
- The benefits of an omniscient POV — 22
- The limitations of an omniscient POV — 22
- Good practice: Deeper knowledge than third-person narration — 23
- Good practice: World-building backstory in a flash — 25
- Good practice: Social commentary and satire — 25
- Good practice: Multiple introductions — 26
- Good practice: Freedom to roam quickly — 28
- Good practice: Tension — 29
- Recommendation — 30

7. Viewpoint drops: Head-hopping — 31

- Overview — 31
- Holding viewpoint in third-person limited storytelling — 31
  - Anaylsis: Tight third-person limited narration — 32
- What head-hopping would look like — 32
  - Analysis: Confused narration — 33

Why head-hopping spoils fiction	34
1. Head-hopping renders a story less immersive	34
2. Head-hopping diminishes suspense	35
3. Head-hopping is less authentic	35
4. Head-hopping can be confusing	36
Write for the page, not the screen	36
Example: What viewers see on the screen	36
The problem: Confused viewpoint in a novel	37
The fix: Singular immersive viewpoint in a novel	38
Head-hop check	39
Viewpoint characters: What the reader can access	39
Non-viewpoint characters: What the reader can access	40
Examples	40
Recommendation	40
8. Viewpoint drops: Motivation we shouldn't have access to	**42**
Overview	42
Example 1	42
Example 2	43
Good practice: Pulling intention back to the POV character	44
Good practice: Letting the reader work out motivation	44
Good practice: Let the POV character work out motivation	45
Recommendation	45
9. Showing how non-POV-characters are feeling	**46**
Overview	46
Showing rather than telling emotion	46
Quick tips to unlock non-POV character emotion	47
Good practice: Shown emotion in published fiction	48
Recommendation	49

10. Viewpoint characters versus protagonists	50
Overview	50
Protagonists	50
Viewpoint characters	50
Is the protagonist always the viewpoint character?	51
Applying the terminology: An example	51
Recommendation	55
11. Closing thoughts	57
The terminology of storytelling	58
Cited sources	61

1. What is narrative point of view?

Point of view (POV) describes whose head we're in when we read a book ... from whose perspective we discover what's going on – and the smells, sounds, sights and emotions involved.

There can be multiple viewpoint characters in a book and multiple viewpoint styles. To complicate things, editors' and authors' opinions differ as to which approach works best, and what jars and why.

This guide reviews the most-oft-used POVs, and explains each one's advantages and limitations. We'll also look at the effect on a reader's engagement with character and story when viewpoint is confused.

POV can be tricky to the uninitiated. My aim is therefore to keep the guidance as straightforward as possible, not because I think you should do it only this way or that way, but because most people (myself included) handle complexity best when they start with the foundations and build up and outwards.

Why should you bother nailing POV?

Pro editors and experienced writers agree on one thing: it's worth the beginner author's and editor's time to understand POV so that they can make decisions about which works – and where and why – and when revision is required.

A better read

The right POV in the right place enriches the reader's experience; the opposite will mean your book is not as immersive as it might have been. It might even confuse or frustrate your reader. I'm assuming you want your book to be the best it can be, so understanding how narrative POV works, and how to use viewpoint with intent, will help you in that endeavour.

A better price

If you're a writer working with a professional editor, whether a story-level editor (developmental, structural editing) or a sentence-level editor (line editing, copyediting, proofreading), there'll be less to fix if your POV doesn't jar. And since viewpoint problems are time-consuming to fix, you're likely to get a better price.

A better fix

Some beginner authors, for reasons of budget, choose not to work with a developmental editor. This is the shaping stage in which decisions about how POV should ideally be handled. If you go straight to working with a line editor or copyeditor, and they encounter major POV problems, it's likely that their editing will have to be more invasive than either of you would have liked. Plus, the fix might not be as elegant as it would have been if any problems had been attended to before the sentence-level work began.

5 narrative viewpoint styles

There are multiple ways in which to narrate a novel. Some are more popular than others, and some easier to master. What you choose will shape not only the story you tell but also your readers' understanding of it. The options are as follows:

- First person
- Second person
- Third-person limited (also called third-person subjective)
- Third-person objective
- Third-person omniscient

Up next ...

The next chapter looks at first-person narratives – what they are, why they work, and what their limitations are.

2. First-person POV

Overview

First-person narrative POVs are the most intimate, the most immediate, but they're less flexible. The pronouns used are 'I' and 'we'.

The benefits of a first-person POV

The reader is privy to an individual character's thoughts, emotions and experiences, all told through a distinctive voice. We see, hear, smell and feel what the character sees, hears, smells and feels. We are compelled to move through the story knowing only what they know, and at their pace.

First-person narratives are rich because they mimic intimate conversations. Imagine you're sitting in a room with someone, just the two of you, and they're telling you about a profound experience. That 'I' on the page is therefore immersive.

The limitations of a first-person POV

Care needs to be taken if this viewpoint style is used throughout an entire novel, from the point of view of only one character.

Too much 'I' can be laborious to read and can result in a told, reported narrative rather than shown prose.

Furthermore, readers can access only one version of events, which can render the prose restrictive if it doesn't allow for the telling of other interpretations; we are forced to trust that the narrator's telling is reliable. Furthermore, if the unveiling of how, why and when is too slow, the story could begin to drag.

Good practice: Not relying on 'I'

It is possible to write a first-person narrative that's engaging. In *To Kill a Mockingbird* (p. 5), Harper Lee keeps 'I' to a minimum and yet the prose oozes with first person. Note in particular how the voice is rich and distinct, rather than the more neutral tone we'd expect from third-person objective narration.

> Maycomb was an old town, but it was a tired old town when I first knew it. In rainy weather the streets turned to red slop; grass grew on the sidewalks, the court-house sagged in the square. Somehow, it was hotter then; a black dog suffered on a summer's day; bony mules hitched to Hoover carts flicked flies in the sweltering shade of the live oaks on the square. [...]
> We lived on the main residential street in town – Atticus, Jem and I, plus Calpurnia our cook. Jem and I found our father satisfactory: he played with us, read to us, and treated us with courteous detachment. [...]

Because Lee doesn't append 'I' plus a verb to much of the prose, we are given a shown narrative that *we* can experience rather than being told how the narrator experienced the world being described.

Compare the Harper Lee excerpt with the 'I'-heavy example below (don't worry – I made it up!) and consider how the narrator's told experience keeps the reader at a distance.

> I placed my hand on the rusty handle and tugged, but the old oak door refused to give way to me. I heard a rustling sound behind me and turned my head. I spotted movement in the inky shadows and felt the skin on the back of my neck prickle with terror as I realized I wasn't alone.

Let's rewrite this with a less invasive first-person narration in which the reader can experience the action as it unfolds.

> The handle was rusty against my palms as I tugged but the old oak door refused to give. A rustling came from behind and I turned. A shape flitted in the inky shadows and the skin on the back of my neck prickled. I wasn't alone.

Good practice: Sustaining interest with other interpretations

In *The Word is Murder* (p. 208), author Anthony Horowitz is one of the characters! The viewpoint is first person (his). The author is like a floating camera; we see the protagonist – the detective (Hawthorne) who solves the crime – through Horowitz's eyes as he accompanies him to interviews with suspects and on visits to crime scenes.

The author-character offers his own theories, even pursues his own lines of investigation, and interjects with stories about his life and career. This adds interest but, ultimately, it's the detective who grounds the crime story, brings reliability to the narrative, and drives the novel forward; it's through him that we access the procedural elements and the answer to whodunnit. Here's an excerpt:

> They'd used blue and white tape to create a cordon which began at the front door and blocked off the stairs. I wasn't sure how they would deal with the neighbours on the upper and lower floors. As for me, although I hadn't been questioned, a woman in a plastic suit had asked me to remove my shoes and taken them away. That puzzled me. 'What do they need them for?' I asked Hawthorne.
>
> 'Latent footprints,' he replied. 'They need to eliminate you from the enquiry.'

Recommendation

First-person narratives introduce depth and explain motivations but can be difficult to sustain if not sufficiently interesting and there's too much told narrative. Watch out for filter words if you think you're over-telling.

Consider whether your whole novel needs to be in first person. Perhaps limiting this approach to specific characters in dedicated chapters would be more effective. If you decide to stick with first person throughout, think about voice and how your viewpoint character (and therefore the reader) will discover the how, when and why of the story at an engaging pace.

And, finally, if you're basing your whole novel in the first person, be cautious about using the present tense throughout. The past might give you more flexibility, particularly if you're writing action-heavy scenes where, in reality, the character wouldn't have time to give much thought to the consequences and motivations of their behaviour.

Up next ...

The next chapter focuses on second-person narratives. We'll look at why they're powerful and the challenges they present for the writer and the reader.

3. Second-person POV

Overview

In second-person narrative POVs, the pronoun is 'you'. This narration is intimate, but strangely so, as if the author is talking directly to the reader *as a character*. That intrusive element is both its strength and its weakness.

It's powerful because it places readers at the heart of the story, and yet we – the 'you' – know less than the narrator. That can create a sense of immediacy, but almost amnesiac dislocation. We have to discover what we think, see, know and do. And if we don't identify with the 'you' – if we feel implicated rather than attached – we can be pulled out of the story rather than drawn in deeper.

The benefits of a second-person POV

This controlling aspect of second person can have an advantage. Whereas first-person narrators tell you what *they* thought and did, second-person narrators tell us what *we* thought and did. This witnessing adds a level of reliability (even if we don't like it). And readers aren't daft. They know they're not really the you-character, which means authors could use it as a tool to create surprise when the 'you' is unveiled later in the book.

If you want your readers to feel connected but controlled, second-person POV might be just the ticket.

The limitations of a second-person POV

Second-person viewpoint is difficult to pull off and it's rare that authors of contemporary commercial fiction write an entire novel in this narration style. More likely, you'll see shorter-form use: dedicated chapters either in narrative form or written as diary entries, letters or other missives.

Good practice: Tension in a transgressor narrative

The following excerpt isn't actually a second-person narration style – it's a deep first person. However, I've included it here so you can see the power of a distinct but anonymous first-person voice that nevertheless makes the 'you' the focus character.

In *I See You* (p. 176), Clare Mackintosh punctuates her primary third-person narrative (a police officer's) with an anonymous predator's voice, though she keeps the narratives distinct by giving them their own chapters. The distinct transgressor voice explores the predator's twisted psyche intimately, and in a way that enables the reader to understand their motivations – what's making them think and behave so monstrously.

> Now that you know what I do, you're intrigued, aren't you? You're wondering what information I've collected about you; what's listed on my ever-growing website. You're wondering if you'll be stopped, like this girl, by an attractive stranger. You're wondering if he'll ask you out for dinner. [...]
>
> Life's a lottery.
>
> He might have something entirely different in mind for you.

The chapters given over to the transgressor provide a rich sense of cat and mouse when juxtaposed with the more distanced police-procedural storyline. Note how the predator-narrator in the above example bends their perceptions into a warped reality – there are no maybes here; they've decided that this is the way things are and justify their actions accordingly.

Because Mackintosh uses the present tense for her second-person narrative, she's able to retain tight control over the unveiling. We're right in the now of the novel. It's deeply suspenseful, but emotionally demanding to read. However, this narrative style doesn't dominate the novel. The transgressor chapters are shorter, and readers are allowed breathing space as they're pushed gently back into the less intimate third-person narrative of the protagonist.

Good practice: Curiosity, reliability and the complicit reader

In this example from *Complicity* (p. 9), Iain Banks uses the second-person viewpoint in which a narrator reports on the actions and thoughts of an unnamed serial killer addressed as 'you'.

> There is another faint crunching noise as the body spasms once and then goes limp. Blood spreads blackly from his mouth over the collar of his white shirt and starts to drip onto the pale marble of the steps. [...]
> You go downstairs and walk through the kitchen, where the two women sit tied to their chairs; you leave via the same window you entered by, walking calmly through the small back garden into the mews where the motorbike is parked.
> You hear the first faint, distant screams just as you take the bike's key from your pocket. You feel suddenly elated.
> You're glad you didn't have to hurt the women.

Think about how you feel as you read this. It's as if *you're* being addressed, as if *you're* complicit. At the very least, the prose arouses curiosity – who is this 'you', and how is it that the narrator knows so much about them?

Banks doesn't present the novel fully in second person; these sections fall between those of a first-person viewpoint character, journalist Cameron Colley. As such, readers are confronted by a juxtaposition of Cameron's version of events and what was witnessed by the narrator.

Good practice: Tight, witty prose but an acquired taste

In *Half Asleep in Frog Pajamas*, Tom Robbins uses a second-person narration style to take us on a roller-coaster ride of a weekend following a stock-market crash. I've included this excerpt because it's illustrates the challenge of handling self-reflective constructions: 'Nothing about yourself annoys you quite so much as your voice.'

> "Belford, please," you hear yourself plead. Somehow, the alcohol has distanced you from your voice just enough so that you can listen to it as if it had been prerecorded. Still, you can't be entirely objective about it. Nothing about yourself annoys you quite so much as your voice. This is the way, you think, a package of Hostess cupcakes would sound if a package of Hostess cupcakes could speak. Q-Jo, on the other hand, says your voice is your lone saving grace. She claims you are the only career woman she has ever met for whom Dental Drill was not a second language.

The whole novel is in second person, and while Robbins' prose is funny and whip-sharp, it is demanding, relentlessly so. Like Marmite, some readers will struggle with it; others will gladly go along for the ride. Think about whether you'd want to read 80,000 words in this narration style. Then think about what percentage of your possible readership would.

Recommendation

By all means experiment with second-person point of view but understand its implications. If you want to draw your reader into the heart of your story, it's a good choice. However, that connection can come at a price – a lack of control that could alienate your audience. Overdoing it, says James Peacock, 'can feel like a form of harassment from someone trying too hard to get into your head'.

For that reason, consider the purpose of this narrative style and the extent to which you employ it. It might be better constrained – limited to chapters inhabited by specific viewpoint characters.

If in doubt, rewrite your scene in an alternative narrative viewpoint so you can evaluate how this affects your perception of the story as a reader.

Up next ...

Now let's look at third-person limited, a popular narration style that readers are used to and comfortable with.

4. Third-person limited POV

Overview

Along with third-person objective, this viewpoint is the one that most writers find easiest to master at the beginning of their journey. Furthermore, readers are used to encountering it in contemporary fiction. The pronouns of choice are 'she', 'he', 'it' and 'they'.

The benefits of a third-person-limited POV

Third-person limited is so called because it's a deeper viewpoint that limits readers to a single character's experience – what they see, hear, feel and think. Readers get to sit in their skin and that provides an immersive experience. It's as if we're them.

However, it's called third-person *limited* for a reason. Strictly speaking, what that character can't see or know shouldn't be reported.

Third-person limited is effective because an author need not give everything away at once. The limitations over what can be known, and therefore divulged, allow the writer to control the unveiling of information via the viewpoint character. We journey with them, which means writers can introduce suspense and tension.

The limitations of a third-person-limited POV

Third-person narration can end up reading flat in the hands of writers who are prone to exposition – telling rather than showing character experience.

> She realized that these were piles and piles of carefully folded foil packets held in dozens of clear plastic bags.
> She didn't need to know what was in them. Drugs of some kind, she thought. Nothing she wanted to know about. (*She Lies in Wait*, pp. 26–7)

'She realized that these were' and 'She didn't need to know' detract from the immediacy of the prose. Just because we're writing in third person doesn't mean we always need to include the subject of the sentence. The beauty of a limited narration is that we're in that character's head, which in this case means we know it's 'she' doing the realizing.

Let's recast, removing the clutter – the realizing and knowing that act as filters, dilute the character's voice and increase the narrative distance. Notice how the prose now has more punch to it. We can imagine that character being hit by the realization of what she's seeing, the shock of it, the desire to unknow, unrealize. It's emotional, and it's no longer just the viewpoint character's experience; it's ours too.

> Piles and piles of carefully folded foil packets held in dozens of clear plastic bags.
> Drugs of some kind. Nothing she wanted to know about.

Another restriction of third-person limited is the very thing that gives it power: the necessary investment in a single character's experience. Because, as readers, our perspective is limited, we can immerse ourselves in the character for the section or chapter so that they become what Mittelmark and Newman call 'our second self'. When we're pulled out of that space and forced into another character's head:

> 'It gives the feeling of a fleeting and unexplained moment of telepathy, an uncomfortable intrusion of somebody else's thoughts. When the protagonist's point of view resumes, we move forward into the narrative warily, ready at any moment for a fresh assault on our minds.' (Mittelmark and Newman, p. 159)

It means the reader's trust has been lost. We'll review this in more detail in Chapter 7 but here's a short example that demonstrates how things can go wrong. Jan is the viewpoint character.

> Jan ran down the road, her lungs screaming for air. She snatched a glance over her shoulder, hoping to Christ Melody was behind.
>
> 'You okay, Jan?' said Melody. She'd barely got the words out – her throat was on fire. All she wanted to do was stop, breathe, devour that bottle of water in her backpack bouncing hard against her spine.
>
> 'We're here,' Jan said. Thank God. Tears of relief stung her eyes. She'd been worried Mel wouldn't keep up. Guilt niggled. Would she have gone back for her? She wasn't sure.

All is well and good in the first paragraph. Jan is our 'second self'; we feel her screaming lungs and hope that Melody is behind. Then we're in Melody's head, our throats as parched as hers. Then we're back in Jan's head, experiencing her worry and her guilt. We don't know which character to invest in, and we're more likely to stop caring about them and the story.

Good practice: Intimacy and getting under the character's skin

Here are some examples from Mick Herron, Harry Brett and Louise Penny that demonstrate an intimate third-person limited narrative:

> For almost a minute that was that. Shirley could feel her watch ticking; could feel through the desk's surface the computer struggling to return to life. Two pairs of feet tracked downstairs. Harper and Guy. She wondered where they were off to. (*Dead Lions*, p. 17)

> His mum pushed past him, bringing a cloud of thick night air seasoned with salt and something he couldn't place. A perfume perhaps, but not his mother's normal scent. (*Time to Win*, p. 321)

> The blurred figures at the far end of the long corridor seemed almost liquid, or smoke. There, but insubstantial. Fleeting. Fleeing.
> As she wished she could.
> This was it. The end of the journey. Not just that day's journey as she and her husband, Peter, had driven from their little Québec village to the Musée d'Art Contemporain in Montréal, a place they knew well. Intimately. (*A Trick of the Light*, pp. 1–2)

The voices are distinctive. It's not just dialogue that conveys how the viewpoint characters speak and think; it's the narrative too. In the above examples, we're left with questions – of destination in the first, of the origin of a smell in the second, and of the nature of the journey – because we don't know any more than the viewpoint characters.

Good practice: Third-person limited in the present tense

I love this example of a tight third-person narrative that gets us right inside the head of Ruth, the viewpoint character. The author uses free indirect speech in the first and last sentences of this excerpt, so that we're shown her thoughts without being *told* she's thinking.

> Honestly, isn't one Bronze Age body enough for him? It's one more than he has ever discovered. But, despite her irritation, Ruth secretly shares his hope that there might be more bodies buried under this soil. The position of the skeleton and the presence of beaker pottery indicate that this was a formal ritual burial. Could this be a barrow cemetery? *The Ghost Fields*, p. 5)

Recommendation

Stick to a single character's POV within each chapter or section to avoid confusion or interruption. It will make your writing life and easier and your reader's ability to invest in their second selves smoother.

Watch out, too, for exposition: too much 'she' or 'he' and filter words that tell of realization, wondering, thinking, knowing. Instead, mix things up with free indirect speech. It retains the third-person narration style but holds the essence of first person and is therefore immersive.

Up next ...

The next chapter focuses on third-person objective point of view, another popular narration style that writers can use when they want to increase the distance between reader and character.

5. Third-person objective POV

Overview

If third-person limited provides intimacy – allowing us to explore a character's emotions and hear their voice – third-person objective offers a more neutral flexibility when we need some distance to look around and beyond.

Like its limited sister, writers find this easier to master than first, second or omniscient narration, and readers are used to encountering it. The pronouns are 'she', 'he', 'it' and 'they'.

The benefits of a third-person-objective POV

It's a useful viewpoint for the author who wants to convey descriptive information and set a scene – height, weight, facial expression, behaviour, and the environment. If you're using this POV, practise your *observation* skills so that you understand how people move from place to place, what they wear, where they live, how they gesture, so that you can show what might be going on in their heads through *what can be observed.*

Here's a quote from Stephen King's masterclass at the University of Massachusetts Lowell.

> 'We begin by observing ... you have to look. You have to see. You can't just walk and let it all go by ... you've got to see how people are, you've got to look for the person who, when they eat, they have a tendency to look down at their plate and they're tearing their napkins ... or somebody who's in a cafeteria and they've kind of like got the straw in pieces ...'

The same can be said of the objects in your novel. How does light play on water or a brick building at various times of the day? What sounds might be audible in your environment? How do the seasons affect the flora and fauna?

Third-person objective viewpoints are powerful because they force a writer to show rather than tell what's being seen. That's because we're not accessing the internal thoughts, feelings and motivations of a character.

Another advantage of this narration style is that it gives the reader a break. Being stuck within a character's head can feel claustrophobic, especially if they're traumatized. Objectivity allows us to focus on the what and where rather than the how and why.

That has advantages when it comes to mystery and suspense too, because the reader is allowed to create their own emotional responses to the reportage rather than being encumbered by a character's perspective.

It's also a good tool when an author wants to keep things moving: action scenes, fight scenes, escape scenes. Here the pace is faster and characters' emotional reactions might be so invasive has to moderate the pace.

The limitations of a third-person-objective POV

Third-person-objective viewpoints are a step back. And because narrative distance between reader and character is wider, it can leave prose feeling flat if overused. Yes, we understand how things appear, but we don't know the reasons, the motivations, the emotional responses – the story behind the story.

For this reason, contemporary commercial-fiction writers rarely write entire novels from an objective POV because it's reportage and we can't get into the characters' heads. It's harder to understand what motivates them unless they express it through dialogue. A blend of limited and objective is a more likely choice.

Good practice: A more distant and descriptive narrative

Here's an example from thriller writer David Baldacci that demonstrates third-person narration as observable description.

> Amos Decker trudged along alone. He was six-five and built like the football player he had once been. He'd been on a diet for several months now and had

> dropped a chunk of weight, but he could stand to lose quite a bit more. He was dressed in khaki pants stained at the cuff and a long, rumpled Ohio State Buckeyes pullover that concealed both his belly and the Glock 41 Gen4 pistol riding in a belt holster on his waistband. (*The Fix*, p. 3)

Notice how we're not quite the 'second self' of third-person limited here. Yes, we know things only Decker could know – that he's been on a diet, that he's sporting a belly and a gun under his sweater – which means he's still the viewpoint character, but the tone of the prose is more distant. We're able to look *at* him, see what others might see.

Good practice: Shown-not-told narratives in action

Here are some excerpts from Stephen King's *The Stand* that demonstrate a close attention to the way things and people behave when observed.

> The Chevy jumped like an old dog that had been kicked and plowed away the hi-test pump. It snapped off and rolled away, spilling a few dribbles of gas. The nozzle came unhooked and lay glittering under the fluorescents. (p. 8)

> "Clock went red," the man on the floor grunted, and then began to cough, racking chainlike explosions that send heavy mucus spraying from his mouth in long and ropy splatters. Hap leaned backward, grimacing desperately. (p. 11)

> She walked softly up behind him and laid both hands on his shoulders.
> Jess, who had been holding his rocks in his left hand and plunking them into Mother Atlantic with his right, let out a scream and lurched to his feet. Pebbles scattered everywhere, and he almost knocked Frannie

off the side and into the water. He almost went in himself, head first. (p. 16)

Objectivity allows the writer to explore in detail what would be unnatural for a character to report directly. Remember, we're not accessing thoughts, opinions and emotions with an objective POV, just the stuff that any onlooker could see, hear or smell.

Objective is the key word here. Third-person objective viewpoints should focus on what could be known by a narrator witnessing that scene. When information is reported that moves beyond a floating camera that's tracking the immediate environs and into a space where the narrator knows more than could possibly be witnessed by the character or the onlooker, omniscience is in play.

In some genres – crime fiction for example – this can be useful because the reader will be forced to reach their own conclusions as to the reasons for, or motivations behind, a particular event or behaviour. In other words, it's mysterious and suspenseful.

Good practice: Blending objective and limited

In the first paragraph of the example below, David Baldacci uses third-person objective to give us background facts. In the second, he switches to limited to explain the character's feelings. It's a lovely fusion:

> His size fourteen shoes hit the pavement with noisy splats. His hair was, to put it kindly, dishevelled. Decker worked at the FBI on a joint task force. He was on his way to a meeting at the Hoover Building.
>
> He was not looking forward to it. He sensed that a change was coming, and Decker did not like change. He'd experienced enough of it in the last two years to last him a lifetime. He had just settled into a new routine with the FBI and he wanted to keep it that way. (*The Fix*, p. 3)

Good practice: Tension-filled objective prose

Notice the dramatic tension in the following excerpt. At no point does the author report anything other than what can be seen ... until the final sentence, when the word 'carefully' shifts us gently away from our more distant objective position and into the viewpoint character's head. It's an excellent example of shown prose – Barry and Helena must surely be afraid, desperate and in terrible pain, but the rich objective narration allows us to do all the imagining for ourselves.

> He sheds the fire-burned parka and snow pants and takes the chair beside Helena, who's already typing on the keyboard as quickly as her scorched fingertips will let her, blood running out of the corners of her mouth and eyes.
>
> As she begins to strip out of her winter clothes, Barry goes to the cabinet and takes the only remaining skullcap that has a full charge. He powers it on and places it carefully on top of his wife's head, which is blistering over. (*Recursion*, p. 311)

Recommendation

Use third-person objective POV to create suspense, to make your reader wonder, ask their own questions, and come to their own conclusions about what's being experienced. Even objective viewpoints can be richly evocative.

Objective narration also gives your readers a breather if emotionality is interfering with the pace of a scene or overwhelming the reader.

And don't be afraid to blend objective with limited narration. As long as you respect the role of the viewpoint character, the shifts between the two narration styles will be seamless.

Up next ...

Now to omniscient, the most challenging of narration styles.

6. Third-person omniscient POV

Overview

This viewpoint is the trickiest to master. Omniscient means *all-knowing*. It's the most flexible because it gives the reader potential access to every character's external and internal experiences. It also has the potential to be the least intimate if not handled well.

The benefits of an omniscient POV

Omniscient is flexible. The narrator knows everything, more than an observer or any of the individual characters – backstory, motivations, intentions, emotions. And in the past, present and future.

'An omniscient narrator,' says developmental editor Sophie Playle, 'could be a character in the story (like a god or an enlightened person), or they could be an observing nonentity.' They'll have their own distinctive voice too, which can be useful if the writer wants to explore the experiences of far-removed environments and focus characters.

The limitations of an omniscient POV

Remember the 'second self' discussed earlier? The removed voice of the narrator, and their omniscient knowledge, makes it difficult for readers to invest emotionally in the focus characters because we're not truly experiencing what they're experiencing. It's always filtered through the all-knowing narrator, who possesses knowledge they don't.

For some genres, that works well, but for others – thrillers and romance, for example – it's often a step too far and dislocates the reader's engagement.

There's also the issue of control to consider. Here's Playle again: 'Completely omniscient viewpoints are difficult to pull off well because the narrator needs to have reasons for imparting the knowledge they choose to impart in the order they choose to do so, otherwise the story will feel contrived.' Readers can end up feeling manipulated, as if the author has opened a back door, revealed something interesting because it's convenient to do so, then slammed it shut when they want to build suspense and hide something else.

Some authors try to mix third-person-limited narrations with omniscient, but more often than not it feels like head-hopping to a reader. If we're accessing one character's thoughts and experiences, made to feel as if they're our 'second self' but are then bounced into another character's head, that's not an all-knowing narrator in play; it's literary version of table tennis, and it jars.

Good practice: Deeper knowledge than third-person narration

If you've read anything by Neil Gaiman, you'll see a blatant external narrator in evidence with a depth of knowledge that defies the rules of a third-person viewpoint. Here's an example from *Neverwhere* (p. 10).

> He continued, slowly, by a process of osmosis and white knowledge (which is like white noise, only more informative), to comprehend the city, a process which accelerated when he realized that the actual City of London itself was no bigger than a square mile [...]
>
> Two thousand years before, London had been a little Celtic village on the north shore of the Thames which the Romans had encountered and settled in. London had grown, slowly, until, roughly a thousand years later, it met the tiny Royal City of Westminster [...]
>
> London grew into something huge and contradictory. It was a good place, and a fine city, but there is a price to be paid for all good places, and a price that all good places have to pay.
>
> After a while, Richard found himself taking London for granted.

The first paragraph might appear to be a third-person viewpoint ('He' refers to Richard, the protagonist), but that's not the case. What follows is a distinct narrative other, a voice that explains 'white knowledge'. In the second and third paragraphs, the all-knowing narrator offers historical information. Then in the final paragraph, we're told more about Richard. The viewpoint was never third-person objective. It was omniscient all along.

In Cormac McCarthy's *The Road*, 'the man' takes centre stage in most of the sections such that we see what he sees and feel what he feels. It's almost as if he's the narrator, and once more we could be forgiven for thinking that the viewpoint is third person. But there's more going on here.

In the following extracts, notice the shift beyond what it's possible for the man to see, think or know.

> He woke in the morning and turned over in the blanket and looked down the road through the trees the way they'd come in time to see the marchers four abreast. Dressed in clothing of every description, all wearing red scarves at their necks. Red or orange, as close to red as they could find. He put his hand on the boy's head. Shh, he said. (pp. 95–6)

> He wallowed into the ground and lay watching across his forearm. An army in tennis shoes, tramping. Carrying three-foot lengths of pipe with leather wrappings. [...] The phalanx following carried spears or lances tasselled with ribbons, the long blades hammered out of trucksprings in some crude forge upcountry. The boy lay with his face in his arms, terrified. (p. 96)

In the first extract, only an all-knowing alternative narrator could be privy to the intent behind the marchers' colour choice of scarves. In the second, the man watches the army, but it's only an omniscient narrator who can know where their blades were forged and how the boy is feeling. Maybe that narrator is McCarthy; maybe it's someone else. But it's not the man.

Good practice: World-building backstory in a flash

Some genres – science fiction and fantasy for example – lend themselves well to omniscient narrators because they can provide critical world-building backstory quickly. Terry Pratchett's *Wyrd Sisters* provides a fine example (pp. 1–2).

> Through the fathomless deeps of space swims the star turtle Great A'Tuin, bearing on its back the four giant elephants who carry on their shoulders the mass of the Discworld. A tiny sun and moon spin around them, on a complicated orbit to induce seasons, so probably nowhere else in the multiverse is it sometimes necessary for an elephant to cock a leg to allow the sun to go past.
>
> Exactly why this should be may never be known. Possibly, the Creator of the universe got bored with all the usual business of axial inclination, albedos and rotational velocities, and decided to have a bit of fun for once.

Good practice: Social commentary and satire

Omniscient viewpoint comes into its own when authors want to pepper their prose with social commentary and satire that's distanced from the belief systems and experiences of their novel's characters.

Let's start with an example from Thackeray's classic, *Vanity Fair* (p. 6):

> Honest Jemima had all the bills, and the washing, and the mending, and the puddings, and the plate and crockery, and the servants to superintend. But why speak about her? It is probable that we shall not hear of her again from this moment to the end of time […]
>
> But as we are to see a great deal of Amelia, there is no harm in saying, at the outset of our acquaintance, that she was a dear little creature; and a great mercy it is, both in life and in novels, which (and the latter

especially) abound in villains of the most somber sort, that we are to have for a constant companion so guileless and good-natured a person. As she is not a heroine, there is no need to describe her in person; indeed I am afraid that her nose was rather short than otherwise, and her cheeks a great deal too round and red for a heroine; but her faced blushed with a rosy health, and her lips with the freshest of smiles, and she had a pair of eyes which sparkled with the brightest and honestest good-humour, except indeed when they filled with tears, and that was a great deal too often; for the silly thing would cry over a dead canary-bird; or over a mouse, that the cat haply had seized upon; or over the end of a novel, were it ever so stupid.

Thackeray uses an omniscient POV to tell us everything his omniscient narrator (or more likely *he*) thinks about his characters, and the rules and norms of the society within which they live. Omniscience allows him to speak directly to the reader, thereby temporarily bypassing the voices of the players, whether those be reliable or not. And with it we are given not historical drama but timeless satire.

Good practice: Multiple introductions

Omniscience can be used to introduce us to a cast of characters – who they are, and what they are doing and thinking. Here's an example from Charles Dickens's *Our Mutual Friend* (p. 671). Dickens uses a seamless omniscient viewpoint to show us the internal and external experiences of Bradley Headstone, his pupils and Miss Peecher.

> The scholars saw little or no change in their master's face, for it always wore its slowly-labouring expression. […] As he paused with his piece of chalk at the blackboard before writing on it, he was thinking of the spot, and whether the water was not deeper, and

> the fall straighter, a little higher up, or a little lower down.
>
> [...] It was evening, and Bradley was walking in the garden, observed from behind by a blind but gentle little Miss Peecher, who contemplated offering him a loan of her smelling salts for headache, when Mary Anne, in faithful attendance, held up her arm.

For a more contemporary example, we can turn to Mick Herron, author of the Jackson Lamb thrillers, a series about MI5 officers who've screwed up and been sent to Slough House to shuffle paper.

Herron doesn't use a god as the lens through which we see. He uses a cat. He imagines our feline friend sneaking 'like a rumour' (*Dead Lions*, p. 9) into Slough House and checking out the various rooms' occupants. Of course, a cat doesn't think or behave with intention like a human. The cat can't possibly know any of the things that we're told during its wanderings. Instead, Herron uses it as a cheeky tool to introduce the cast, the environs, and the atmosphere of Slough House.

Dead Lions is Book 2 of the series. Herron wants to introduce us to a cast of characters, most of whom appeared in Book 1. However, he respects the fact that not all his readers will have read the first book, and that those who have might have forgotten who these people are and why they're important.

The omniscient POV allows him to do the introductions quickly and cleanly, and democratically. None of the characters are explored in depth. Rather, Herron gives us a snapshot of what he wants us to know about them, what makes them tick.

> Louisa would have gone onto her knees, gathered the cat in her arms and held it to her quite impressive breasts – and here we're wandering into Min's area of opinion: [...] breasts that are just right; while Min himself, if he could get his mind off Louisa's tits long enough, would have taken a rough manly grasp of the cat's scruff; (p. 11)
>
> And while our cat would have crossed this threshold as unobtrusively as it had all the others, that

wouldn't have been unobtrusive enough. River Cartwright, who is young, fair-haired, pale-skinned, with a small mole on his upper lip, would immediately have ceased what he was doing – paperwork or screenwork; something involving thought rather than action, which perhaps accounts for the air of frustration that taints the air in here [...] (p. 12)

And here's an example from Gaiman's *Neverwhere* (p. 8). In the second paragraph, the omniscient narrator blatantly interrupts the story to give us some character description.

> So Mr. Ross went first, in his filthy T-shirt and his crusted blue jeans, and Croup and Vandemar walked behind him, in their elegant black suits.
> There are four simple ways for the observant to tell Mr. Croup and Mr. Vandemar apart: first of all, Mr. Vandemar is two and a half heads taller than Mr. Croup; [...] fourth, Mr. Croup likes words, while Mr. Vandemar is always hungry. Also, they look nothing at all alike.
> A rustle in the tunnel darkness; Mr. Vandemar's knife was in his hand, and it was quivering gently almost thirty feet away.

Good practice: Freedom to roam quickly

Let's return to Herron. Through the imaginary cat, we're given the freedom to roam without intrusion. No single character's feelings or experiences dominate over the others. It's a form of speedy literary democracy.

That roving feline shows us not only key details about each character, but also how they perceive each other. That's difficult to do with first-person and third-person narration without offering lengthy and interruptive explanations of how the information was acquired.

But when our cat pokes its head round the door, it'll find only Ho. The office is his alone, and Ho prefers this, for he mostly dislikes other people, though the fact that other people dislike him back has never occurred to him. And while Louisa Guy has been known to speculate that Ho occupies a place somewhere on the right of the autism spectrum, Min Harper has habitually responded that he's also way out there on the git index. [...] (p. 10)

It's a lucky escape for our cat [...] for on this particular morning the nigh-on unthinkable has happened, and Jackson Lamb is not dozing at his desk, or prowling the kitchen area outside his office, scavenging his underlings' food; nor is he wafting up and down the staircase with the creepily silent tread he adopts at will. He's not banging on his floor, which is River Cartwright's ceiling, for the pleasure of timing how long it takes Cartwright to arrive [...] (p. 13)

Good practice: Tension

The omniscient can convey a sense of tension that sets up the next scene. Back to Herron. The main man, Jackson Lamb, head of ops, is not in residence. And that's unusual. Rather than hopping from one internal monologue to another, or cluttering the text with dull dialogue in which the various characters express their confusion about their boss's absence, the omniscient narrator tells us in only eighteen words ('Simply put ...') that everyone knows he's absent, and no one knows why.

[...] and he's not ignoring Catherine Standish while she delivers another pointless report he's forgotten commissioning. Simply put, he's not here.
And no one in Slough House has the faintest idea where he is. (p. 13)

The narration throughout this section is distant, devoid of emotion. It's literally a cat's-eye view.

Recommendation

I'd recommend caution. The beauty of fiction often lies in the unveiling, in the immersion. Overuse of an omniscient narrator can block this.

The all-seeing eye can be a powerful tool – as demonstrated by the examples above – but less experienced authors, particularly those writing commercial fiction such as romance, thrillers and mysteries, risk accidental head-hopping, which will destroy the tension and distance the reader from the characters.

Up next ...

The next chapter explores head-hopping in more detail, and why it causes disengagement.

7. Viewpoint drops: Head-hopping

Overview

Head-hopping is in play when readers are forced to bounce from one character's head to another in the same scene. Unless the narration style is omniscient – which, as we've already discussed, is a tricky beast to master – head-hopping can dislocate a reader from a story.

Holding viewpoint in third-person limited storytelling

Take a look at this excerpt from *In a House of Lies* by Ian Rankin (p. 16). It's a solid example of third-person limited viewpoint.

> Rebus pushed open the wrought-iron gate. No sound from its hinges, the garden to either side of the flagstone path well tended. Two bins – one landfill, one garden waste – had already been placed on the pavement outside. None of the neighbours had got round to it yet. Rebus rang the doorbell and waited. The door was eventually opened by a man the same age as him, though he looked half a decade younger. Bill Rawlston had kept himself trim since retirement, and the eyes behind the half-moon spectacles retained their keen intelligence.
> 'John Rebus,' he said, a sombre look on his face as he studied Rebus from top to toe.
> 'Have you heard?'
> Rawlston's mouth twitched. 'Of course I have. But nobody's saying it's him yet.'
> 'Only a matter of time.'
> 'Aye, I suppose so.' Rawlston gave a sigh and stepped back into the hall. 'You better come in then. Tea or something that bit stronger?'
> […]
> 'Sugar?' Rawlston asked. 'I can't remember.'

> 'Just milk, thanks.' Not that Rebus was planning on drinking the tea; he was awash with the stuff after his trip to Leith. But the making of the drinks had given him time to size up Bill Rawlston. And Rawlston, too, he knew, would have been using the time to do some thinking.

Anaylsis: Tight third-person limited narration

Rebus is the viewpoint character. That means the internal experiences we access are limited to his. For example:

- We see through his eyes: the well-tended garden, the bins, Rawlston's half-moon specs and intelligent eyes.
- We hear through his ears: the silent hinges on the garden gate.
- We think what he thinks: sizing up Rawlston as he makes tea.

We cannot get in Rawlston's head. All we can do is consider his internal experiences via his observable and audible behaviour, and his dialogue. For example:

- His mood is gloomy – shown by the dialogue 'Tea or something that bit stronger?' and what Rebus can see: the sombre expression.
- He's riled by Rebus's question – shown by the dialogue 'Of course I have' and Rebus's observation of the twitching mouth.
- He begrudges letting Rebus in – shown by the dialogue 'You better come in then' and what Rebus hears: the sigh.

What head-hopping would look like

Here's what that excerpt might look like if head-hopping was in play:

Rebus pushed open the wrought-iron gate. No sound from its hinges, the garden to either side of the flagstone path well tended. Two bins – one landfill, one garden waste – had already been placed on the pavement outside. None of the neighbours had got round to it yet. Rebus rang the doorbell and waited.

Bill Rawlston walked down the hall and peered through the peephole. Rebus. Same age as him, though he looked half a decade older. He opened the door.

Rawlston had kept himself trim since retirement, and the eyes behind the half-moon spectacles retained their keen intelligence.

'John Rebus,' he said, a knot forming in his stomach as he studied Rebus from top to toe.

'Have you heard?'

The question riled him. Was Rebus stupid? 'Of course I have. But nobody's saying it's him yet.'

'Only a matter of time.'

'Aye, I suppose so.' Rawlston begrudged letting Rebus in but stepped back into the hall. 'You better come in then. Tea or something that bit stronger?'

[…]

'Sugar?' Rawlston asked. 'I can't remember.'

'Just milk, thanks.' Not that Rebus was planning on drinking the tea; he was awash with the stuff after his trip to Leith. But the making of the drinks had given him time to size up Bill Rawlston.

Rawlston had used the time to do some thinking, too. Rebus turning up here after all those years – it pissed him off.

Analysis: Confused narration

Notice how we bounce between the heads of Rebus and Rawlston. Now we have access to the internal experiences of both.

- We're in Rebus's head as he pushes open the gates and reports on the silent hinges, the well-tended garden and the bins. Then we're in Rawlston's as he walks down the hall, identifies Rebus and reports on his appearance.
- We bounce back to Rebus's head as he observes Rawlston's trim figure and intelligent eyes.
- Rawlston speaks, and the action beat throws us back into his internal experience – the knot of anxiety in his stomach. The dialogue continues and we remain in Rawlston's head, learning of his annoyance with Rebus's question.
- Rebus asks for milk and we bounce back to his head – discovering that he has no intention of drinking the tea but has used the time to size up Rawlston.
- Finally, we hop over to Rawlston one more time, where we learn that he's sized up Rebus too and is angry.

In that butchered version, the reader is forced to play a game of ping-pong on the page.

Why head-hopping spoils fiction

Here are four reasons why holding viewpoint is preferable to head-hopping. I've used the Rankin example as a reference point.

1. Head-hopping renders a story less immersive

In Rankin's original prose, we are limited to the world of the novel as Rebus experiences it. That's powerful because every word on the page is a step we take with Rebus, as Rebus. I get to be a male, Scottish detective for a few hours rather than a female, English book editor!

In my butchered version, I take that first step with Rebus but then trip and fall into Rawlston. Because I'm bouncing between those characters' internal experiences, I don't have time to invest in either. And so I stay as lil' ol' me. I do like being me, but when I buy one of Rankin's books I want to immerse myself in its world for a few hours at a time and dig deep under the skin of the viewpoint character. I can be me without paying fifteen quid for the privilege!

2. *Head-hopping diminishes suspense*

In the original text, Rankin keeps the suspense tight by allowing us to access only Rebus's senses. Rawlston's sombre expression, twitching mouth and curt responses make Rebus (and us) think, Does he want me here? Does he begrudge my presence? What's going on in his head?

Those questions demand answers and we seek them in the clues offered by the limited narrative. Because the limited viewpoint requires Rebus and the reader to make assumptions based on what's observable and audible, there's uncertainty. That's what provides the suspense, and it compels us to keep reading in the hope that the truth will be unveiled.

In my head-hopping version, the prose is flat. There are no questions. We know what everyone's thinking because we're in everyone's head. Readers aren't called upon to use their imagination – both characters' internal experiences are spoon-fed to us.

3. *Head-hopping is less authentic*

Head-hopping reminds readers that they are in a story written by an author. We don't get to suspend belief because the writing won't allow us to immerse ourselves that deeply.

In Rankin's original prose, we walk through the world as if we are Rebus, and Rebus alone. That's what happens in real life. I know only what I'm thinking, feeling, seeing and hearing. I can't be sure than another's perception is the same. Audio-visual signals help me make reasonable assumptions but I'm only ever in my own head ... or Rebus's if I'm reading a story about him because Rankin knows how to hold viewpoint.

In my mangled version of the excerpt, there's a reality flop. Now I'm everyone, which is ridiculous of course. Authenticity has fallen off a cliff.

4. Head-hopping can be confusing

When a writer head-hops, the reader has to keep track of whose thoughts and emotions are being experienced. When a reader doesn't know where they are in a novel for even a few seconds, that's a literary misfire.

This is what happens in the head-hopping excerpt. For example, Rawlston walks down the hall and identifies Rebus through the peephole. We're right with him, in his head. But what follows is jarring. That he reports on his spectacles sitting in front of keenly intelligent eyes is oddly self-aware.

Of course, it's not Rawlston's perception; it's Rebus's. And once we realize that, the prose makes sense. But working that out is not where Rankin wants the reader's attention. He's telling us a story and he wants us to read it. That's why he holds a tight limited viewpoint throughout.

Write for the page, not the screen

Viewpoint sometimes unravels because a novelist approaches their story as they imagine what it would look like on the screen. Imagine watching this short scene on TV:

Example: What viewers see on the screen

One of the characters, Matt, ducks under a hedge. We seem him grimacing, shutting his eyes tightly. Then the camera cuts to a close-up of the thorns in the hedge pressing into his head. Perhaps there's a trickle of blood down one side of his neck.

The camera stays with Matt and we see him mouth the word 'bitch'.

We hear the clip-clopping of heels, and the camera moves to a lone woman on a footpath in the garden – Adriana. She speaks into her phone, saying, 'He can't have gone far. Find him and take him out,' then rubs her throat. She continues to talk, telling the person on the other end of the line that she'd had a skinful the previous night and is furious about Matt's interference, which is all she needs because she feels like she has cold coming on.

The camera cuts to another character, John. He's wearing black. We hear him reply to her, telling her not to worry, then watch as he peeks over a wall and sees Adriana.

The view shifts to Adriana. She's putting her phone in her pocket. Her expression is one of anger and frustration.

We go back to John. He pulls down a balaclava and moves stealthily towards an area at the back of the house. He's almost invisible in the darkness of the night but we see him in the shadows because the camera shows us where he is.

Now it's back to Matt. He's still hunched up in the hedge, eyes wide, body still.

The camera zooms out so that we can see Adriana moving ever closer to where Matt's hiding. She's getting nearer.

The view moves in on Adriana. We see her flinch and purse her lips. She hobbles just a little, then bends to adjust her shoe. The camera view tilts down to her feet and we see the redness of the skin where it's rubbing against her stilettos.

The camera cuts to Matt, still in the hedge. But now he's smiling, enjoying Adriana's discomfort.

Notice that the viewer can't know what anyone's *thinking* unless we are told through dialogue or facial expression. Gesturing will fill in the gaps. A soundtrack will also create mood.

The problem: Confused viewpoint in a novel

What some beginner writers do is render the scene in a way that partially mimics the screen version. That's because they're familiar with how stories are presented on the TV or in film.

> Matt ducked under the hedge beside the footpath. He counted silently, mouthing the words, focusing attention away from the hawthorn piercing the back of his neck and scalp. Heels clicked on the footpath close by. Adriana. Bitch.
> 'He can't have gone far. Find him and take him out,' she said. Her throat felt swollen. 'Dammit, and to make things worse, I feel like I've got a cold coming on. Plus, I had a skinful last night.' And she'd

> needed it after that interfering prick Matt had started sticking his nose where it wasn't wanted.
> 'I hear you, Adriana. Don't worry, we'll find him,' said John. He was standing by the north wall, clad head-to-toe in black. Hands grasping brick and flint, he hauled himself up and peeked over to see Adriana pocketing her phone. He pulled down his balaclava and stole south to cover the back, masked by the shadow of night.
> Adriana was on the phone, Matt realized. That was good. It meant she was on her own.
> Adriana continued down the path, getting closer to where Matt was hiding with every step. Patrolling the grounds in stilettos had been a bad idea. They were killing her feet.
> Matt hoped so, after what she'd put him through.

The problem is that there are multiple viewpoints that force the reader to bounce from one character's experience to another; head-hopping. We never invest in Matt, Adriana or John because as soon as we try to immerse ourselves in the experience of one of those people, we're dragged into the head of another.

The result is a wonky head-hopping hybrid of novel and screenplay. We know what everyone's doing, thinking and seeing. It rips out the tension and destroys the structure of the scene.

The fix: Singular immersive viewpoint in a novel

If, however, the writer commits to the viewpoint of *one* character, the prose is very different. In this version, we lose John completely. Adriana is visible but only from Matt's perspective. We don't have access to her thoughts, only what Matt thinks might be going on in her head based on what he knows, sees and hears. He's our 'second self'.

It's shorter, certainly, but the tension is back and the writing is tighter.

> Matt ducked under the hedge beside the footpath. He counted silently, focusing attention away from the

hawthorn piercing the back of his neck and scalp. Heels clicked on the footpath close by. Adriana. Bitch.

'He can't have gone far. Find him and take him out.'

Her voice was thick, like she was full of virus or hungover. Or maybe it was fury.

Matt heard a reply – a man speaking – but the sound was muffled and tinny.

She must be on the phone. That was good. She was on her own. For now.

Patent-black stilettos passed no more than a metre in front of him. The skin below both Achilles looked swollen and red. Those shoes must be killing her, he thought. He hoped so, after what she'd put him through.

Head-hop check

Make a list of the characters in a chapter or scene. Identify the viewpoint character.

There can be more than one viewpoint character in a book but most commercial-fiction authors separate them by chapters or sections. Here's a quick way to check whether you're holding viewpoint.

Viewpoint characters: What the reader can access

- Emotional responses
- Thoughts
- What they can see
- What they can smell
- What they can hear
- What they can touch
- What they can taste

Non-viewpoint characters: What the reader can access
- Observable behaviour: their movements, expressions and gestures
- Audible behaviour: their speech, breathing noises (panting, rasping, retching, etc.) and vocal gestures and tics (sighs, gasps, grunts, etc.)

Examples
- The narrative can tell readers that the milk tasted sour on the viewpoint character's tongue. A likely response to that sourness must be shown for a non-viewpoint character. E.g. they retch and spit out the milk, or report the sourness via dialogue.
- The narrative can tell readers that the viewpoint character has a bellyache or feels a roiling in their stomach. A likely response to the pain must be shown for a non-viewpoint character. E.g. they groan or hold their abdomen, or report the pain via dialogue.
- The narrative can tell readers that the viewpoint character feels excited. A non-viewpoint character's excitement must be shown. E.g. their neck and cheeks flush.
- The narrative can tell readers that a viewpoint character doesn't believe in the tooth fairy. A non-viewpoint character's disbelief must be shown. E.g. they scoff, laugh, sneer, or report their scepticism via dialogue.
- The narrative can tell readers that a viewpoint character thinks they're going to be sick or feels nauseous. The non-viewpoint character's symptoms of nausea must be shown. E.g. their skin changes colour, they grab a bowl, they bend over the toilet, or report the nausea via dialogue.

Recommendation

Even if your readers don't know what head-hopping is, by removing it from your novel you'll give them a more immersive, suspenseful and authentic journey through the world you've built. Plus, you'll ensure they're reading your story, not trying to work out who's telling it.

Up next ...

In the next chapter, we'll look at prose that tells readers what non-viewpoint characters' motivations are, and why that's a viewpoint drop.

8. Viewpoint drops: Motivation we shouldn't have access to

Overview

There's one little word – just two letters – in a narrative that can cause a POV drop: 'to'. Watch out for its use in alongside a non-POV character's actions because it's often an indication of intention and motivation, both of which are internal experiences and are by rights the domain of the viewpoint character.

The constructions you should look out for in relation to a non-POV character's actions take a number of forms, including:

- [did/does X] in an attempt to [verb]
- [did/does X] in order to [verb]
- [did/does X] so as to [verb]
- [did/does X] to [verb]
- [did/does X] because she/he [verb]

Example 1

> I jump over the wall and land on the soft verge. Dan's German shepherd greets me. The dog bares its teeth, preparing to bite.

I'm the viewpoint character. All is well until I meet the dog. It bares its teeth. We're still good. But then the infinitive slips in, and with it I'm now privy to the dog's intention – to bite. It's a step too far. That might not be right; perhaps the dog's been trained to snarl or maybe it's more a warning than an impending attack.

What's important here is that we're not in the dog's head so we can't know its intention. A recast that shows what happens, rather than telling what might, is in order so that viewpoint is held. It might go like this if the scene demands I get bitten.

> The dog bares its teeth, leaps forward and clamps its jaw around my arm, puncturing the skin.

Or like this if I'm to remain injury-free:

> I jump over the wall and land on the soft verge. Dan's German shepherd greets me. The dog bares its teeth and I freeze. It backs off, so I give it a wide berth and trot down the road.

Example 2

> Matty. The guy was a pain, had done nothing but hold her back all day. Denise shoved him hard in the back. He grabbed the side of the boat to steady himself.

Denise is the viewpoint character. We have access to her thoughts via the free indirect discourse: 'The guy was a pain'. That Matty grabbed the side of the boat is fine. In fact, it's a solid example of shown prose because although we don't have access to his intentions or motivations (because we're not in his head) we can make a good guess at what they are from his observable action – grabbing the side of the boat.

However, the infinitive 'to' tells us *why* he grabbed the side of the boat. And that's a problem because we can't know; we're not in his head. All we can do is see through Denise's eyes. Yes, it's likely that he's steadying himself, but why not let the reader do the work? His actions are enough to show them.

A recast might look like this:

> Matty. The guy was a pain, had done nothing but hold her back all day. Denise shoved him hard in the back and he grabbed the side of the boat.

Or this more staccato version:

Matty. The guy was a pain, had done nothing but hold her back all day. Denise shoved him hard in the back. He grabbed the side of the boat.

Good practice: Pulling intention back to the POV character

In this example, Richard is a non-viewpoint character whose actions are being observed by the first-person narrator.

> Richard's cross-examination is short, as if he doesn't think the witness is worth spending a lot of time with. He talks about the bleeding that would take place after the initial splatter, and how blood that was virtually pure could have pooled on the ground. (*New Tricks*, p. 304)

The author could have written 'Richard's cross-examination is short because he doesn't', but that would have been telling Richard's intention and therefore a viewpoint drop. Instead, 'as if he' places the action back in the POV's character's head space – it's his perception.

Good practice: Letting the reader work out motivation

In this example, Fred is the viewpoint character.

> Fred told his legs to move, to go to her and embrace her, but at first they wouldn't obey. It was Ollie who moved, but before he could get to her, Arlene picked up the chicken and threw it. Ollie ducked. The chicken flew end over end [...] (*The Outsider*, p. 99)

Notice that we're not told why Ollie ducked (to avoid the poultry missile heading towards him). That would be a viewpoint drop. Instead, Stephen King allows the action ('ducked') to show the reader what Fred can see, and make assumptions about the intention behind the action.

Good practice: Let the POV character work out motivation

In this example, the narration style is first person. Paul is a non-viewpoint character.

> Suddenly Paul rushed at me, a strange expression on his face. I felt a flicker of panic as his arm reached out towards me – I swerved to avoid it, but he grabbed hold of me. For a terrifying second I thought he was going to throw me off the roof. Instead, he pulled me towards him.
> 'You're too close to the edge,' he said. 'Stay in the middle, here. It's safer.' (*The Silent Patient*, p. 269)

The author does tell us about the viewpoint character's motivation for the swerve – which is fine because we're in his head – but the motivation behind Paul's rushing at and grabbing him is at first mysterious. The POV character's fear that Paul's intention is sinister builds suspense. Only through the shown action and dialogue that's unveiled at the end of the excerpt do we come to understand the true motivation.

Recommendation

Avoid telling readers why non-viewpoint characters are acting as they are. Instead, show their behaviour, and trust the reader to make sense of the cause and effect.

If the motivation for their actions is complex, and not obvious from the shown behaviour, have the viewpoint character ask themselves questions or experience confusion. Even if they can't resolve the truth of the motivation, the search for answers will be immersive and suspenseful.

Up next ...

In the next chapter, we'll look at how to show non-viewpoint characters' emotional states in narrative without head-hopping.

9. Showing how non-POV-characters are feeling

Overview

Non-viewpoint characters have emotions too. But how do we show them without dropping viewpoint, and without using dialogue? We're back to the issue of mastering observable behaviour. Showing rather telling is the key to rich, observable emotion. The shown behaviour needn't be reams of description – it could be an action beat with just a few words, one of which is a strong verb.

Showing rather than telling emotion

Showing what the viewpoint character can see – and their interpretation of that behaviour – allows readers to enter the emotional and physical space of a non-viewpoint character.

In the following excerpt, Jack is the viewpoint character and the narration style is third-person limited.

> The pebble bounces on the water seven, eight, no, nine times. Best ever, Jack thinks.
> Pete weaves through the grass and slumps into a hollow in the dune. His brother's whoop, the arc of his arm ... just like Dad's when they played skimming stones. Before the accident. Before the world changed. He shakes the memory from his head. Dwelling on that stuff never ends well.
> Jack turns away from the ocean, waves and calls for Pete to come down but the crashing surf swallows his words.

There are two things to notice here:

- *Best ever* is Jack's thought. That puts us in his head, which is fine because this is an excerpt from a chapter in which he's the viewpoint character. But that means we cannot access what's going on in Pete's head – how he is

– 46 –

remembering his dad and the accident, and the decision to not dwell on those things.
- Look at the physicality too. Jack turns away from the water, which means he was facing it and couldn't have observed Pete weaving through the grass and slumping into the dune. All he can do is see Pete on the dune after he's turned.

If we recast the scene, we can show Pete's mood, but through *Jack's* eyes.

> The pebble bounces on the water seven, eight, no, nine times. Best ever, Jack thinks.
> He whoops and turns his back to the ocean. Pete's lumbering gait is unmistakable. He weaves through the grass on the dune and slumps into a hollow, mouth set in a hard line, neck hunched into his shoulders, complexion pasty. But he's out; the sunlight's on his face. It's the first time since a month of whenevers.
> Skimming stones was something they did with Dad. Before the accident. Before the world changed. Jack shakes the memory from his head. Dwelling on that stuff never ends well. He waves, calls for his brother to come down but the crashing surf swallows his words.

We don't leave Jack's head. I've given him the memory of their dad and the accident, and the decision to not dwell. I've changed the order of movement, too. Jack turns first so he can observe Pete's journey through the grass and into the hollow of the dune. And Pete's mood shown through the set of his mouth, the position of his neck and the hue of his skin as Jack perceives it. Furthermore, we can infer that he's been struggling to deal with the accident through Jack's relief that he's at least outside for a change.

Quick tips to unlock non-POV character emotion

Think about how non-viewpoint characters' movements, actions and gestures might reflect their internal experience. Showing those, rather than how they feel or think, or what's motivating them, will unlock their emotionality. In the following examples, all the actions can be experienced by the viewpoint character through sight and sound.

- Showing rather than feeling pain: They grimace; clutch a part of their body; wince; howl
- Showing rather than feeling shock: They jump back; gasp; stumble; put a hand to their chest
- Showing rather than feeling anxiety: They fidget with a zipper; pick at their nails; shred a beer mat; stutter
- Showing rather than feeling embarrassment: They blush; avoid eye contact; their breathing is shallow; they speak faster than usual
- Showing rather than feeling nausea: Their complexion is tinged a different colour; they gag or retch; their voice is flat

Good practice: Shown emotion in published fiction

Below are five excerpts featuring non-viewpoint characters. Note how at no point are we allowed into these characters' heads. Despite not being able to access to their thoughts or feelings, their states of mind can be glimpsed through what the viewpoint characters observe and report.

> Marie paused, her shoulders slumped. She spoke without looking up from the floor. (*29 Seconds*, p. 332)

> Old George had sunk to his knees on the muddy ground, sobbing and clutching at his woolly cardigan. (*The Ghost Fields*, p. 120)

> Ralph opened the door, but Samuels put a hand on his arm, shook his head, and raised his eyes slightly to the camera in the corner with its small red light. (*The Outsider*, p. 53)

> Pletnev blew out his breath and wiped his red face with a scrap of towel, dropping the ax into a tree stump. (*Eon*, p. 367)

> 'Certainly,' Ragle said. [...] His eyes, red-rimmed and swollen, fastened on her compellingly; he had taken off his tie, rolled up his shirtsleeves, and as he drank his beer his arm trembled. Spread out everywhere in the living room the papers and notes for his work formed a circle of which he was the center. (*Time Out of Joint*, p. 5)

- Marie: ashamed
- Old George: wracked with distress
- Samuels: wants to warn
- Pletnev: exhausted
- Ragle: exhausted and obsessed

Recommendation

If you're writing in a third-person limited narration style, consider what the viewpoint character already knows, what they can observe in relation to a non viewpoint character, and what they could infer from those observations. That will determine what they can report.

What they report allows readers to access the internal experience of the non-viewpoint character through a back door. And while that report will be biased, it *will* be immersive. Plus, you'll have held viewpoint.

Up next ...

In the next chapter, we'll look at the differences between viewpoint characters and protagonists.

10. Viewpoint characters versus protagonists

Overview

Every novel has a viewpoint character and a protagonist. However, they're not necessarily the same person, at least not all of the time. This chapter explores the differences in these two character roles.

Stories usually have multiple characters, and often have more than one major character. However, just because a character has a major role does not make them a protagonist.

Furthermore, stories can be narrated by different characters in a book. Whoever's head the reader is in is called the viewpoint character. However, just because a character is narrating a story does not make them a protagonist or a major character.

Protagonists

We can think of protagonists as having a MACRO role. The protagonist is the person whose experiences drive the story. The novel revolves around them. Readers are usually more connected to them than any other character.

- It's their choices and motivations that affect the direction of the story.
- It's they who are thwarted by obstacles.
- It's they who we root for as they attempt to find resolution.

Viewpoint characters

We can think of viewpoint characters as having a MICRO role. The POV character is the person who internal experiences drive a scene or chapter.

- Through them we access the detail of a scene.
- It's through their lens that we perceive what's going on in the moment.

- We know what they see, hear, believe, feel and report.

Is the protagonist always the viewpoint character?

No, the viewpoint character and the protagonist can be different characters. While your protagonist might often be the POV character, one doesn't always equal the other.

A POV character can be the protagonist, the antagonist, a major secondary character, a minor character, or a bystander who makes but one appearance. As long as it's their head we're in, and they who are reporting the scene through their experience of it, they're the viewpoint character.

Your protagonist, however, is always your protagonist, whether they're in a scene, doing something else somewhere else, or lying unconscious in some back alley.

Applying the terminology: An example

I've used Linwood Barclay's *Parting Shot* to illustrate the distinction between viewpoint character, protagonist, main character and secondary character.

- The protagonist is Cal Weaver, a private investigator. It's his experience that drives the story, his decisions that affect the direction it takes, his journey we invest in. Is he the viewpoint character, too? Often but not always.
- Barry Duckworth is a major character, and he narrates multiple chapters in the book. He is therefore sometimes the viewpoint character but never the protagonist.
- Jeremy Plimpton is a major character and the prime suspect. He is the person Cal is charged with protecting and is often present, yet not a single chapter is offered through his viewpoint. Cal is always the narrator in scenes and chapters where he appears.
- Cory Calder is a secondary character and the antagonist. He pops up more later in the book as the plot thickens. There

are three chapters in which he is the viewpoint character, despite his secondary role.

Here's a breakdown that shows you how Barclay weaves multiple viewpoint characters into the first 17 chapters of the book.

CHARACTER-ROLE KEY	NARRATION-STYLES KEY
PR = protagonist	3PL = third-person limited
MC = major character	3PO = third-person objective
SC = secondary character	1P = first person

Ch/Sec	POV char	Role	Style	Notes
1	Cal Weaver	PR	1P	We start the book by meeting our protagonist, Cal. The first-person narration style places the reader firmly in his head. We're in his mind, experiencing his thoughts, emotions and senses with him.
2	Barry Duckworth	MC	3PL	We meet new viewpoint character, a detective called Barry. His chapters are always narrated in third-person limited. There's a smattering of free indirect style – third-person narration that has the essence of first person – such that even though the pronoun used is 'he', the reader still sees, hears, thinks and feels along with Barry. Multiple chapters are offered from this major character's viewpoint.

3	Cal Weaver	PR	1P	—
4	Barry Duckworth	MC	3PL	—
5	Cal Weaver	PR	1P	—
6	Barry Duckworth	MC	3PL	—
7	Cal Weaver	PR	1P	—
8	Barry Duckworth	MC	3PL	—
9	Cal Weaver	PR	1P	—
10/A	Monica Gaffney	SC	3PO	The reportage feel of the prose means it's only just obvious that we're experiencing the world through Monica's lens.
10/B	Monica Gaffney	SC	3PL	In this section, we're drawn deeper into Monica's emotional experience – a third-person-limited narration through which we access her thoughts.
10/C	Albert Gaffney	SC	3PL	We shift to a new viewpoint character, that of Albert Gaffney (Monica's father). The limited narration allows us to access an emotional response (e.g. 'He steeled himself').
11	Barry Duckworth	MC	3PL	—

12	Cal Weaver	PR	1P	—
13	Trevor Duckworth	SC	3PO	Now we're in the head of Barry's son, Trevor. The third-person narration style is objective for the most part, but firmly rooted in Trevor's experience.
14	Brian Gaffney	SC	3PL	The POV character is now Brian, Monica's brother. The author enhances the third-person limited narration with free indirect speech (e.g. 'It sure was nice to get out of the hospital. Even though his family had come to see him, the visit had stressed him out.') to narrow the narrative distance between the reader and the character, and root us in Brian's head.
15	Barry Duckworth	MC	3PL	—
16	Cal Weaver	PR	1P	—
17	Barry Duckworth	MC	3PL	—

It goes on until the final chapter wraps up with Cal's first-person viewpoint. We are in his head as he recalls critical information that enables him to put it all together and verbally reveal whodunnit to his audience.

There are 65 chapters in total, each with distinct viewpoint characters narrating the scene. As each viewpoint character takes a turn, they show us what's happening through their actions, emotions, thoughts and senses. The characters – major and secondary – play a variety of key roles:

- Some, the Plimpton family members for example, enrich the fabric of this fictional world by exposing the dirt beneath the shiny surface, and seeding clues that could provide motive.
- One places obstacles in Cal's way that thwart his (and our) understanding of who the guilty party is and threaten his and Jeremy's safety.
- Some are Cal's allies. They ground the story and provide authenticity. For example, Barry and his police procedural work.
- One – Jeremy, the suspect in Cal's charge – helps us root for Cal because a deeper exploration of his character enables us to doubt his guilt and support Cal's quest to discover the truth.

However, there is only one protagonist. It is Cal's job throughout to discover who did what, and why. Even when he's not in the scene, and therefore not the viewpoint character, he's driving the direction of the story, the goal of which is to understand how a young girl came to die.

Recommendation

Take care not to confuse the terms 'major', 'protagonist' and 'viewpoint'. Those attributions don't mean the same thing. To summarize:

A novel can have multiple viewpoint characters, each taking a turn to narrate part of the story. Their viewpoints will enrich the tale but their overall goals don't underpin it. The viewpoint character could be the protagonist, the antagonist, a major character, or a secondary character. As long as they're narrating, they're the viewpoint character.

A novel will usually have only one protagonist. They might be the viewpoint character throughout, in which case we only ever see the world through their lens. Or they might be temporarily absent and allow others to tell a part of the tale and share their emotions and experiences.

A novel will usually have other major and secondary characters whose experiences are central to the story. They might get a chance to narrate the story and therefore be the viewpoint character, or their experiences might be narrated by someone else.

11. Closing thoughts

Know who your viewpoint characters are, choose POV with intention, and recognize the benefits and limitations of each style.

There's nothing wrong with experimenting, and you need not stick to one viewpoint style within a novel, as demonstrated by Mackintosh and Banks. Switches like these can add interest and tension, heighten conflict, and help readers build varying levels of intimacy with different characters.

Do, however, be consistent. Recall how Banks separates his first- and second-person narrations into distinct chapters and sections, and how the choice of narrative style is applied consistently to the viewpoint characters. Doing otherwise will lead to reader confusion. Even if your readers don't know what head-hopping is, by removing it from your novel you'll give them a more immersive, suspenseful and authentic journey through the world you've built. Plus, you'll ensure they're reading your story, not trying to work out who's telling it.

Take care to craft words for the page, not for the screen. Keep the boring stuff out, even if it's realistic. You'll reduce your wordcount but enhance reader engagement.

And look to books written by your favourite novelists for inspiration on how to build a beautiful page, not their Netflix adaptations. Your writing will be all the better for it.

The terminology of storytelling

Action beats are short descriptions that come before, between or just after dialogue.

Adjectives are words that describes nouns.

Adverbs and **adverbial phrases** are words that describes a verb.

Anaphora is the deliberate repetition of words or phrases at the beginning of successive clauses for artistic effect.

Asyndeton is a literary device through which a sentence's structure follows the following pattern: A, B, C (not A, B, and/or/but C).

Character arc describes how a character changes and develops through a story.

Dialogue is the characters' speech.

Dialogue tags, also called **speech tags**, are words that indicate which character is speaking (e.g. Jake said; she said; he asked).

Exposition is the introduction of information. When poorly executed and overblown it can be boring and distracting.

Filter words are verbs that tell us how a character is accessing experience rather than showing us what they're experiencing (e.g. 'noticed', 'realized', 'seemed', 'spotted', 'saw').

Free indirect speech, or **free indirect style**, is a literary device through which viewpoint character voice is resonant. The base tense and third-person narration style are retained but the prose has the essence of a first-person, present-tense thought.

Head-hopping is a narrative misfire in which readers are forced to jump from one character's perspective (thoughts and experiences) to another's. It's a viewpoint problem.

Narrative distance, sometimes **called psychic distance**, describes how close the reader feels to the narrator. When a novel is being narrated by a particular character (for example, in first-person and third-person limited narrations), it will describe how connected we feel to that person and their experience.

Narrative means story. It's the part of the book that's isn't dialogue.

Narrator refers to the person telling the story. It could be one of the characters or an external voice.

Non-viewpoint characters are any other characters in a scene or chapter whose behaviour can be observed or heard or discussed. We don't have access to their internal experience (thoughts, emotions, knowledge, motivations, intentions, and so on).

Omniscient point of view is a narrative style in which the reader accesses the story through the eyes of a distinctive, external all-knowing narrator as opposed to a single character.

Overwriting is characterized by too many words on the page. It's often characterized by repetition and redundancy, and sometimes by a verbose narrator who doesn't trust the reader to do a lot with a few nudges.

Point of view, **viewpoint** and **POV** are used interchangeably to describe whose head the reader is in when they read the story, whose perspective we experience the story through.

Polysyndeton is a literary device through which a sentence's structure follows the following pattern: A and B and C (not A, B, and C; or A, B and C).

Pronouns are words that replace nouns (e.g. I, you, he, she, we, me, it, this, that, them those, myself, who, whom).

Purple prose is overblown, poorly structured writing with strings of extraneous and often multisyllabic adjectives and adverbs.

Quotation marks or **speech marks** indicate the spoken word. Singles or doubles are acceptable but authors and editors should enforce consistency.

Shown prose relates characters' experience through actions and sensory information.

Similes are explicit comparative figures of speech introduced to make description more vivid (e.g. she hissed like a snake, he stood like a statue, they were quiet as mice)

Third-person limited refers to a narration style in which the internal experiences (thoughts, feelings, motivations etc.) of a single character – the viewpoint character – are related.

Told prose relates characters' experience through exposition (the introduction of information rather than actions and sensory information).

Verbs describe doing. They can refer to physical actions (e.g. digging), mental actions (e.g. wondering) or a state of being (e.g. is, are).

Viewpoint characters are the characters whose perspectives we experience as we read: what they think, feel, understand, know, see, hear, and smell.

Word dumps or **information dumps** describe poorly executed exposition – description that lacks sensory detail. They're often a feature of overly told prose.

Cited sources

29 Seconds, TM Logan, Zaffre, 2018
A Trick of the Light, Louise Penny, Three Pines Creations, 2011
Complicity, Iain Banks, Abacus, 1994
Dead Lions, Mick Herron, John Murray, 2017
Half Asleep in Frog Pajamas, Tom Robbins, Random House, 2002
How Not to Write a Novel, Howard Mittelmark and Sandra Newman, Penguin, 2009
I See You, Clare Mackintosh, Sphere, 2016
I'm talking to you: second-person narratives in literature, James Peacock, Keele University, 2018
Neverwhere, Neil Gaiman, William Morrow Paperbacks, reprint edition, 2016
New Tricks, David Rosenfelt, Grand Central Publishing, Reissue edition, 2010
Parting Shot, Linwood Barclay, Orion, 2017
The Fix, David Baldacci, Pan Books, 2017
The Ghost Fields, Elly Griffiths, Quercus, 2016
The Outsider, Stephen King, Hodder, 2018
The Road, Cormac McCarthy, Picador, 2009
The Stand, Stephen King, First Anchor Books, mass-market edition, 2011
The Word is Murder, Anthony Horowitz, Arrow 2018
Time Out of Joint, Philip K. Dick, Vintage, 2002
Time to Win, Harry Brett, Corsair, 2017
To Kill a Mockingbird, Harper Lee, Arrow Books, 1989
Vanity Fair, William Makepeace Thackeray, Wordsworth Editions, 1992
What's the Difference Between Omniscient and Third Person Narration?, Sophie Playle, Liminal Pages
Wyrd Sisters, Terry Pratchett, Harper, reprint edition, 2013

Printed in Great Britain
by Amazon